Dennis Taaffe

The Probability, Causes, and Consequences of an Union

Between Great Britain and Ireland,

discussed: with strictures on an anonymous pamphlet, in favour of the

measure, supposed to be written by a gentleman high in office.

Dennis Taaffe

The Probability, Causes, and Consequences of an Union Between Great Britain and Ireland,
discussed: with strictures on an anonymous pamphlet, in favour of the measure,
supposed to be written by a gentleman high in office.

ISBN/EAN: 9783337298159

Printed in Europe, USA, Canada, Australia, Japan

Cover: Foto ©Suzi / pixelio.de

More available books at **www.hansebooks.com**

THE
PROBABILITY, CAUSES, AND
CONSEQUENCES

OF AN

U N I O N

BETWEEN
GREAT BRITAIN and IRELAND,

DISCUSSED:

WITH STRICTURES ON AN

ANONYMOUS PAMPHLET,

IN FAVOUR OF THE MEASURE,

SUPPOSED TO BE WRITTEN BY A GENTLEMAN
HIGH IN OFFICE.

By the rev. DENNIS TAAFFE.

DUBLIN:
PRINTED BY J. HILL, 51, ABBEY-STREET.—1798 ·

PROBABILITY, CAUSES, AND

CONSEQUENCES

OF AN

UNION, &c.

AMIDST the difgrace and ruin brought upon us
by the late unfortunate events; by the intole-
rant pride and avarice of fhort-fighted monopoly
on one hand, holding in its greedy grafp the exclufive management of a mutilated conftitution, as
an engine of exclufive dominion and fpoil; and the
intemperate zeal and ambition of thofe who fought
reform, and through reform looked for equal freedom, union, national government, and the general
profperity of all, without diftinction of fect; at-
tainable, as they fuppofed, through the medium of
a virtuous independent legiflature, reprefenting the
entire nation. Amidft the general mourning and
defolation that fadden our plains, the cries of deftitute widows and orphans, the bleeding recollec-
tion of the moft horrible cruelties and atrocious
crimes, plunder, maffacre, torture, fanaticifm, and
all the furies recorded in fable or hiftory; amid
the grief, terror, and anxiety that benumb the

A

heart, and palfy the intellectual powers; the def-
pondency of the good, the dreadful licence of the
wicked; the heart-burnings and deadly animofity
that rankle in the breafts of men fmarting from recent injuries, and breathing nothing but revenge,
even to extermination; while all freedom of enquiry, whether by fpeech or writing, is treated as
treafon, and ftruck dumb by the terrors of martial
law and military execution; it may be deemed rafh
to come forward with any political opinion, at a
period fo inaufpicious to truth and juftice. It may
be deemed an hopelefs tafk to awaken the public
mind to national concerns.

Amid the general difmay that affumes the ap-
pearance of apathy, I for one am ready to acknowledge, that I do not defpife exiftence, deftitute as
it is of moft thofe circumftances that render it de-
firable, and beguile the burthen of life. The al-
luring profpects that fafcinate youthful ambition,
the gay, the charming delufions that give an intereft to the moft trivial objects of defire, that enli-
ven the fpirits, and fire the fancy, on our entrance
in the career of human affairs, are fled indeed. I
can no longer cherifh life for the fake of any felfifh plan of individual happinefs; one ftrong motive furvives, the defire of promoting the happinefs of my kind, and of doing fomething ufeful in
my day. Have I performed my tafk? or is my
death likely to prove more beneficial to mankind,
than my further continuance in exiftence? I truft,
in that cafe, the trying hour fhall find me chearfully
refigned to the ftroke. I was not made to cringe
and fawn to ruffian power, for the wretched purpofe of obtaining a permit to live at the expence
of truth, and the duty I owe my countr and man-

kind; and moſt of all, to tyrants and their accomplices, for ſurely none ſtand ſo much in need of the wholeſome admonitions of truth, as the deluded victims of paſſion and injuſtice, who hate her moſt.

It is a duty incumbent on us to miniſter to the wants of our fellow-creatures, moſt eſpecially their moral wants. When the word Tyrant is mentioned, ſome perſons are apt to confine its meaning excluſively to the abuſe of eſtabliſhed authority. That however is a groſs miſtake. Coercion exerciſed on others by any force, in the place of argument or perſuaſion, comes properly under that denomination. The pike of the inſurgent may be as much in the ſervice of tyranny, as the bayonet of the mercenary. Force in any ſhape is a very improper inſtrument of conviction; it may put a temporary reſtraint on the external man, but the hoſtile mind ſtill remains. Every purpoſe that is honeſt will be beſt promoted by amicable diſcuſſion, from whoſe mild beams no men or meaſures can ſhrink, without pleading guilty by the very fact.

Away with the rage and folly of faction; its criminal exceſſes, its brutal unmanly triumphs in the diſgrace and ruin of our country. Had the men of blood a particle of intellect; did any thing humane, or civilized, or patriotic enter into their compoſition, they would bewail, with tears of blood, the calamities they have inflicted on themſelves, as well as on their ſuppoſed enemies, and the undefinable evils they have prepared for our common poſterity. They have acted in the very manner their worſt enemies could wiſh. What ſpectacle would the enemy of Ireland wiſh to be-

hold that he has not feen? Irifhmen divided into
hoftile factions, tearing the bowels of their country, cutting each other's throats, and firing each
other's habitations! Whoever ftimulates them to
mutual ftrife and ruin, muft expect to make them
both a prey; their divifions will facilitate fuch an
enterprize, and they will fpeedily reap the fruits
of their wickednefs and folly, in the lofs of that
conftitution which they preconized and abufed;
and in the irrevocable doom of provincial fervitude, one party invite a French invafion, the other
invite a Britifh invafion. The latter have fucceed-
ed, and will no doubt keep what they have conquered. It were a filly dream to imagine that Britifh arms effected the conqueft of Ireland for the
benefit of Orange-men; that blood was fhed, and
Englifh treafure wafted, out of pure good will for
Irifh proteftants.

The Britifh cabinet laughs at our party diftinctions; while it openly profeffes to cherifh that party which promotes its views, it can fee no other
merit in it than its fubferviency. 'Tis not as Irifhmen, furely, that they can flatter themfelves to
poffefs the partial favour of Englifhmen. On what
occafion then? As proteftants. Oh! filly bigots!
How little do you comprehend the expanded views
of the illuminated minifter. He can league himfelf juft as cordially with emigrant papift priefts,
with popifh Auftria, and inquifitorical bigot Spain,
to advance his own fchemes; he would league
himfelf with the Turk, Jew, Pagan, or even the
devil himfelf, for the fame end.

When all Ireland was catholic, expedients were
found to create and keep alive a Britifh faction.
was If it all proteftant now, fome new contrivance

would not be wanting, fome paltry ridiculous diftinction, to anfwer the purpofe of dividing the
people, and forming a faction fold to foreign intereft, and hoftile to the foil. Or fuppofe the proteftants formed the great majority of Irifhmen, and
felt it their greateft intereft to fupport the independence and profperity of the country; and that the
catholic minority were as eager to become the tools
of Britifh fupremacy as the proteftant now is, they
would meet with the fame kind of favour, encouragement, and reward, as the mifnamed afcendancy now receives; they would, like the prefent pot-
wallopping dogs, be permitted to lick the crumbs
that fell from the table of Britifh fupremacy.

Irifhmen, you have fealed your own doom. The
moment you appealed to foreign powers, and in-
voked the interpofition of foreign force in your
domeftic difputes, you have proclaimed your inability to govern yourfelves ; you have renounced
your independence, your autonomia or felf-legifla-
tion, fo dearly purchafed. You became the vaffal
of that power which has *protected* you againft each
other, and thus you verify the old proverb, " A
houfe divided againft itfelf cannot ftand." Num-
berlefs are the inftances on record of this truth;
Poland and Ireland ftand laft on the lift. Afcendancy or Orange, whichfoever name you like beft,
your unwearied efforts fhall be crowned with their
merited reward. The blefllings you refufed to
fhare, and which by fharing you would encreafe an
hundred fold, are about to elude your felfifh gripe.
Your little pride, with your little delegated tyranny, and divifion of fpoil, are at the laft gafp, for
an UNION with Britain now occupies the attention of the Britifh cabinet!

This meafure has long been in contemplation.
Now that we are on the eve of feeing it realized,
we ftand amazed! affect to look on the report as
unworthy of belief, and fcarcely allow ourfelves to
difcufs the probability or confequences of fuch an
event. This conduct is ftupid. We fhould pre-
pare ourfelves for the approaching crifis, and make
up our minds as to the conduct we fhould hold;
whether to approve or condemn, to fupport or oppofe the meafure.

To that end I beg leave to offer what has occur-
red to me on the fubject, ftating the arguments on
each fide of the queftion with as much impartiality
as I am capable of. For the fake of perfpicuity, I
fhall divide the fubject under the following heads:

1ft. Is the union of legiflatures practicable or
probable at this day?

2d. Is it likely to prove beneficial to this country
or otherwife?

The firft propofition naturally refolves itfelf into
the two following:

1ft. Has the Britifh minifter the means of ac-
complifhing it?

2d. Does it appear defireable in his eyes?

As to the firft queftion of the fecond divifion, it
is eafily folved. His ability to accomplifh it is in-
difputable. With large Englifh armies in the heart
of our country, and more ready to follow in cafe
of need, yet he finds his fureft refource in our
own divifions! Such is the miferable ftate to which
thefe fatal feuds have reduced us, that we can oppofe no effectual refiftance to any meafure, however inimical to our profperity. It remains then to
examine, whether the meafure in queftion fhall appear a good one. Mr. Pitt would not hefitate to

anſwer in the affirmative. Let us ſketch the reaſons he would probably urge in defence of it.

"In her preſent ſituation Ireland cannot be ſuffered to remain. What is ſhe at the preſent hour? A mere burthen on us; inſtead of contributing her contingent towards this moſt expenſive and juſt war in ſupport of eſtabliſhed governments, ſhe drains us of men and money; her diſtractions alarm and agitate us; they depreſs our funds, and encourage the hopes of our vigilant enemy, by preſenting him with a vulnerable part, in which the empire may be aſſailed with ſucceſs. The reputation of our government has ſuffered in the eyes of Europe, by reaſon of the atrocities perpetrated there in its name. My conſcience acquits me of any participation in the foul deeds. If I call on our party there for ſupport, I do not invite them to be brutal. I commanded no rapes, or robberies, or tortures, nor burning of houſes, nor maſſacres of unconvicted felons. If I ordered them to ſubdue and ſuppreſs, I did not require of them to exterminate, and that with the moſt horrible circumſtances of diabolical cruelty and baſe-hearted villainy. I iſſued no orders to aſſaſſinate every one they met, whether innocent or guilty, if not poſſeſſed of the private ſignals of Orangiſm.

"This maſs of evil, phyſical and moral, that affect ſo eſſentially the honour and proſperity of the empire, might, for the preſent, be conſigned to oblivion, and your preſent ſyſtem of Iriſh government be endured, did not the well founded apprehenſion of the future recurrence of ſimilar diſorders forbid it. [He is ſuppoſed here diſcuſſing the queſtion with the ſelf-appointed Iriſh agents.] If the paſt furniſh any criterion to judge of the future,

we have no great profpect of deriving benefit from
the prefent terms of our connection. What is
your hiftory fince the firft eftablifhment of it, but
a gazette of the wars, maffacres, and devaftations
occafioned by encroachment on the one hand, and
refiftance on the other? Whatever be the caufes of
this misfortune, they have operated hitherto un-
ceafingly. The caufes muft be fought for either in
the natural and incurable depravity of the Irifh, or
in the unfavourable circumftances in which they
were placed. Incredible as it muft feem to a re-
flecting and difpaffionate judge, many have been
the utterers of the former alternative; abfurd, almoft blafphemous calumny, equally difgraceful to
the heart that would conceive, and the head that
could give utterance. Were that the cafe, they
muft be left to themfelves or exterminated!

" But no. Human nature is every where much
alike; fufceptible of every impreffion, good or ill;
of almoft any degree of refinement or barbarity,
virtue or vice. Civilization has made the tour of
the world, and nations have had their viciffitudes,
of civilization and fcience, of ignorance and barbarity. Our anceftors, the painted Britons, were
on a level with the Pagans of the prefent day;
while Egypt, Chaldea, Greece, &c. poffeffed arts
and fciences. Now that Britain excels in all thefe
accomplifhments, what are the defcendants of the
above mentioned renowned nations? Even Ireland
has had her period of learning and civilization! in
a word, mankind are what the civil and religious
inftitutions of the world have made them; toge-
ther with influence of foil, climate, and geographi-
cal pofition.

" Having thus, as I think, cleared the Irifh

character from the malevolent afperfions even of many Irifh writers, over-zealous to defend ruling meafures at the expence of national character, I am free to fix the entire blame of thofe calamities that confume you and injure us, on the defects in your political fyftem. You muft have an afcendancy, as the price of fupporting cur fupremacy. And what is that afcendancy ? A monopoly of all power, honour, public offices, and the emoluments flowing from thence; the power of ruling and taxing the nation at pleafure, and the produce of the whole public revenue, levied upon the people at large, diftributed in the fhape of falaries and penfions among yourfelves and partizans.

" Really your vaunted loyalty to the connexion is purchafed at an enormous price ; it is a mercenary and miferable thing. It is time to confider, whether the fervices you have performed deferve to be requited in this prodigal manner. You may boaft indeed of being the moft able architects of difcontent and confufion in the king's dominions. The tyrannical and infulting manner in which you treated the juft claims of the Irifh, after their expectations were raifed on the feemingly ftrong ground of royal bounty, and their evident expediency and juftice fpread general difcontent, the violent meafures of coercion and oppreffion to which you reforted, contrary to all law and right, in order to fmother complaint, and ftifle the communication of opinion, encreafed the ferment. A banditti of exterminators long paraded through the North in the moft public manner, to the terror and difmay of his majefty's peaceable fubjects, exercifing with entire impunity every fpecies of cruelty and rapine on the defencelefs catholics of Ul-

ſter; all applications to the Caſtle for redreſs or
protection were fruitleſs; and this miſchief was to-
lerated for years, to the utter ruin of thouſands,
and therefore not abſurdly ſuppoſed to have the ſecret ſupport and countenance of g——.

" The catholic peaſantry of Ireland finding no
protection in the laws of the land, combined in
their own defence, and thus two hoſtile aſſociations
overſpread the kingdom; hence the facility with
which republican principles have been propagat-
ed. Long might united Iriſhmen preach republicaniſm in vain to a nation deeply prepoſſeſſed with
prejudices of the moſt inveterate kind, in favour
of monarchy and hierarchy in their moſt deſpotic
ſhape, if inſult and perſecution had not prepared
their minds for innovation; if Jacobins harangued
and wrote, it was g—— procured for them a partial and favourable audience. Thus republicaniſm,
from being confined to a few ſpeculative men,
through the crimes of a—— became the political
creed of the nation.

" The ſecret committee pretends to have done
wonders, by relating the technical forms of the or-
ganization, and a ſketch of the proceedings, with
ſongs and ſymbols, &c. All this was matter of
courſe, expected by thoſe who laid the foundation
thereof. They modeſtly forgot how much the
union was indebted to their own labours for its
formation and extenſion. A diſcerning public will
not ſuffer their modeſty to detract from their juſt
praiſe; it ſees with regret, that the compilation is
incomplete, until the hiſtory of two or three pre-
ceding ſeſſions of parliament, the exploits of O-
range, and other military and civil agents are add-
ed by way of preface.

" Afcendancy prepared difafters for Ireland, and
brought the empire into a fituation full of danger
and difficulty; and this return they make for the
liberal conceffions of England, which made their
parliament nominally independent, but in reality
only encreafed the wages of the party, by bringing
home, as they term it, all the great offices of ftate,
and creating a vaft and novel patronage. Your
pretenfions to retain this fyftem, at a time its in-
competency has been proved to the world, are no
lefs abfurd than unjuft; it is abfurd to pretend to
legifiative independence, while you depend on our
treafure and armies for your very exiftance. It is
unjuft you fhould enjoy the encreafed emoluments
and honours flowing from that independence which
you do not deferve, becaufe you cannot maintain
them.

" True, you have not been as yet overthrown;
but how would ye have fared if left to yourfelves?
It would be better policy not to have provoked the
conflict. What language do you hold at prefent?
You tell the Commons of Great Britain, you muft
fupport us with your money and men, and yet you
muft not pretend to direct our councils; we muft
enjoy legiflative independence. What kind of an
Irifh bull! independent dependance! As well
might the fenator pretend to independence, who
lives by the price of his votes. When the claim of
independence was firft urged, we underftood its
merits; it was backed by a PATRIOT army of un-
bought and free citizens, who fecured internal
tranquillity more by the refpect and gratitude
their patriotifm infpired, than by the application
of the bayonet. Your country was then ftrong in
the union of its inhabitants, happy at home, and

respected abroad ; secure against invasion. Your
government, while pursuing the career of patriot-
ism, appeared every way equal to its functions;
it did not come whining to us for support, and
complaining of the sedition and treason of the people. With reversed fortune, it becomes you to
alter your language, and lower your pretensions.
You tell the people of Ireland support a constitution, from a participation of whose rights and benefits you are excluded; support the monopoly
which crushes, degrades you, and makes you
aliens on your native soil; support that which
makes contempt, slavery, and beggary your inhe-
ritance; support that which brands you as unworthy to share the benefits of civilized society ; and
which, by stripping you of every degree of political consequence, gives you as many tyrants as
there are members of the privileged cast.

" This is the hydra of great and petty tyrants,
that claims your loyalty to its foul usurpations, and
deprives you of all sort of influence that might
secure you from oppression, and make it the interest of men in, or aspiring to power, to treat you
individually or collectively with respect. Men in
a free constitution are secure from oppression, thro'
the interest their fellow-citizens are likely to feel
for their concerns, and this sympathy must result
from some common interest, as the community of
rights; common rights producing a common dif-
position to support those rights, or favour conferra-
ble by the exercise of such rights, as voting, pleading, &c. Thus in a well regulated system of freedom there is a chain of mutual dependance from
top to bottom, that connects all the parts by the
ties of mutual interest, and prevents the least from

[15]

being treated with neglect, or oppreſſed by the
greateſt; the king is obliged to court the commons, thoſe in their turn are obliged to court the
people. If any freeman of the latter deſcription
is injured, he has the ſympathy of his own order,
and the ambition and deſire of popularity preva-
lent among the higher to protect him. But the
unfortunates who ſuffer civil excommunication from
the pale of theſe privileges, are ſubject to inſult
and oppreſſion from all quarters; they are the he-
lots, doomed to toil, torture, or death, at the
pleaſure of their taſk-maſters. It is not merely by
compariſon with the happier lot of their neighbour,
that they muſt feel their ſlavery embittered, it is
really aggravated by additional, and very ſubſtan-
tial hardſhips, over and above what are incident to
the ſubjects of an abſolute monarchy. Under an
abſolute and enlightened monarch, the ariſtocracy
is not allowed to cruſh the laborious claſſes to ſuch
a degree, as would preclude them from the neceſ-
ſaries and comforts of life. Whatever advantage
may fall to the lot of the induſtrious, is open alike
to all. But with you every non-freeman feels himſelf preſſed by an ariſtocracy, or privileged caſt of
his own trade and profeſſion; and from ſome pro-
feſſions, or at leaſt their higher honours, he is entirely excluded.

" There is a gradation of ariſtocracies branch-
ing from the throne to the forty-ſhilling freeholder,
ſqueezing him like the folds of the hydra, and
cruſhing him to the earth. If maſters there muſt
be, as Homer ſays, better have one than many:

Ουκ αγαθη πολυκοιρανια εις κοιρανος εςω.

With all thefe wrongs weighing them down, while
you conceded a little, and left them room to hope
for more in time, they fupported you chearfully;
then you called for free trade and independence,
and you got it. England reaped this advantage
from your union, as fome compenfation for them
conceflions, that fhe was not obliged to protect
you either by fea or land; but on the contrary, received confiderable aid from Ireland both in men
and money. What on the other hand is the fruit
of your prefent fyftem, as impolitic as it is inhuman? Your weaknefs compels you to lean on England for fupport, and thus you contribute to para-
lize her efforts, engaged as fhe is in a moft arduous ftruggle. Your haughty and infulting denunciation of eternal oppofition to juft claims, provoked general difcontent, conveyed in language opprobrious and unmannerly; your meafures of co-
ercive violence, and organized banditti of exterminators and plunderers, fanned the flame into a
civil war.

" Can it appear wonderful, if men thus goaded
beyond the bounds of human bearing, fhould re-
taliate and commit exceffes? They had not the
nature or feelings of man if they did not. Under
its prefent circumftances, you cannot guarantee
the tranquillity of your injured country for a fingle
twelvemonth, nor your own exiftence as a government, without powerful fupport from hence. During fome future, if not the prefent French war,
you are liable to be overthrown, and by your overthrow to bring great calamity on us all. Your
fyftem is burthenfome for the prefent, *...plete with
mifchief and difgrace, and pregnant with the feeds
of future deftruction. Two other modes remain to
be tried, a reform or an union.

" Since my entrance into office, I had always
strong objections to reform, because I began to
view things in a new light; but more than ever
since the French revolution. I now think that a
reform would only give the republicans a purchase,
that would enable them to overthrow the constitution. So much for reform in general. As to a reform in Ireland, it would be attended with the
further inconvenience of leading to the separation
of the two countries. Perhaps alarming as such an
event might seem to some people, it would be better for England than your present condition. Some
politicians are wont to frighten themselves with the
consequences of Irish independence; they dread
much from the commercial rivalry of that favour-
ed country, possessing the full command of its natural resources, and having expatiated on the fer-
tility of her soil, the goodness of her climate, her
numerous bays, harbours, and rivers, her mines,
population, cheapness of labour and provisions;
they ask, how could England support the competition? These are the idle fears of shallow or interested men. Her wealth and luxury would put an
end to relative cheapness, and make her the better
market for our commodities.

" Our rivals the French are, in time of peace,
our best customers, precisely because they are, after Britain, the wealthiest nation in Europe. Even
a connexion of reciprocal interest would cement
the sister islands, in a manner more beneficial to
both than the present. Ireland would then feel
herself interested to preserve England from being
over-run by the arms of France, on the principles
of self-preservation, and the efforts of a people
become wealthy and powerful, and acting on a

conviction of juſtice and neceſſity would be more formidable. The union of nations connected by the ſtrong ties of mutual intereſt has proved laſting and benificial to both parties.

"But let us, for the preſent, diſmiſs theſe views of the ſubject, and conſider the only remaining alternative, viz. an incorporation with Great Britain, and weigh the probable conſequences. At a moment when the great ſtates of Europe are already overgrown in power and territory, it is not for Great Britain to ſit down ſupinely, and ſuffer the diſmemberment of her empire; 'tis rather her policy to incorporate more intimately the circumjacent, and, as it were, the domeſtic members thereof, by drawing cloſer the ties that unite them; this will enable her to protect diſtant ſettlements, and invigorate public credit, by giving additional ſecurities to the public creditor. It will occaſion an influx of wealth into England by the concourſe of rich proprietors, who will reſort hither in crouds from your ſide the water, as the great mart of ambition, elegance, buſineſs, and pleaſure. Finally, it will form an additional barrier againſt the dangerous ſpirit of innovation, by throwing an hundred additional members into both houſes, entirely devoted to the miniſter of the day, which will enable me to apply the redundancy of influence not wanted for the ſervice of the current year, to the formation of a ſinking fund of patronage, towards purchaſing the remaining Jacobinical parts of the conſtitution. Ireland, ſubject to military government, will become a convenient barrack to awe the ſpirit of Jacobiniſm in this country, in caſe it attempts any thing; for theſe reaſons, both government and people will chearfully accept the union.

" As for the consequences likely to refult to Ireland from the meafure, that you mufl acknowledge is
matter of very fecondary confideration; fince that
conquered country ought, in all reafon, exift folely
for our benefit. Let her enjoy her religious quar-
rels, the fanguinary rage of her factions. What
more would fhe have? Does fhe not poffefs Orange-
men, and defenders, and rebels, and loyalifts, proteftants, papifts, prefbyterians, fwadlers, &c. &c.
Are not all thefe indulged in the comfortable fatisfaction of cutting each other's throats for the love
of God, and the virgin Mary, and her fifter Biddy;
or for church or king, as they like beft? How un-
reafonable to grumble after fuch conceffions! with
her hands full of fuch falutary works, your people can never feel the want of employment. The
fuperabundant hands that may be fpared from the
martial and honourable fport of murder, man-hunt-
ing, and ravifhing, may attend the flocks that fatten
for the Englifh market. We fhall have no objecti-
on to fill the ranks of our fleets and armies with
them. I do not prohibit our manufacturers and ca-
pitalifts from fettling among you, if they chufe to
truft their lives and fortunes among the wild Irifh.
Your farmers fhall have to deal only with agents,
ftewards, and middlemen, inftead of the proprietors, which muft redound very much to their fatisfaction, as they have long experienced the lenity
of the former defcription of mafters.'
Here ended the confoling logic of Thaumoturgus.
To which John Paddy, fpeaker, replied in the following manner:
" And is it thus you reward your faithful fervants,
the loyal afcendancy or orangemen? Is it for this
we rifqued our lives and fortunes, and in fact fhed
C

our blood and fquandered our properties ? For you,
ungrateful England, we have oppreffed our country,
deluged it wtih the blood of its inhabitants, over-
run it with fire aud fword for your intereft, and to
gratify your hereditary hatred to the Irifh name
and nation, we have rekindled the decaying fpirit
of bigotry. Wherefore have we armed neighbour
againft neighbour, friend againft friend, relative
againft relative, with rage unprralleled, and put
arms into their hands to affaffinate, and burn, every
plebeian uuinitiated ; to ravifh their wives and
daughters, burn their houfes, &c. Wherefore have
we ranfacked the Englifh language for epithets of
reproach and contumely, to rouze an irritable people to exceffes, and when they did not anfwer the
wifhed-for purpofe, did we not refort to acts of legiflative defpotifm, which proving inadequate, we
adopted the decifive meafure, by ordering military
execution on the people ? Oh ! ungrateful John
Bull ! have we not always acted as your faithful
garrifou, retaining Ireland in your chains for your
profit, enabling you to deprive it of trade, manufactures, and national government ; to turn it into
a draw farm for the fupply of your navy and your
markets ; to drain it of men and money at your
good pleafure ? have we not faithfully and affidu-
oufly co-operated with you, in devifing fuch laws
as might reduce them to a ftate of poverty, barbarity, and ignorance, by depriving them of the means
of induftry, and rendering its acquifitions infecure,
by clofing againft them the avenues of education,
of preferment and wealth ? Could you contrive
more effectually to accomplifh this, than by the fup-
preffion of printing and inftruction in the national
lenguage ? well knowing that before a whole peo-

ple can mafter a ftrange idiom, and renounce their vernacular tongue, many generations muft pafs a-way, during which interval, the want of books and inftruction muft reduce them to complete ignorance. For the fame laudable end, we fupprefled their colleges, and made it penal for them to ftudy abroad. Further, left by any clandefine means they fhould labour to reach the prohibited fruit of knowledge, we ftrengthened our forementioned provifions, with incapacitating ftatutes, difqualify-ing for the exercife of the profeffions, in which learning and ability are difplayed to advantage; thus cutting off every motive that can ftimulate in-duftry, or conduct men to eminence in the career of literature and fcience.

"Do we deferve no credit for thofe ingenious methods of barbarizing mankind, unparalleled in the annals of the world? All this we have achieved for your fake, that you might the more eafily retain them in bondage, fleece and opprefs them with impunity; for you know that knowledge is power, and ignorance is impotence. If Ireland be this day your foot-ftool (to ufe a fcripture phrafe) your pifs-pot, or whatever elfe you chufe to make it; if you may fafely treat its inhabitants as the vileft of flaves, whip them like dogs, fhoot, or hang, or baftile, or condemn them to the gallies, agreeably to your good pleafure, to our labours you ftand indebted for this eminent gratification!

"Oh! were that defpifed people enlightened and united, nor you, nor any power on earth could tread them down on their native foil with impunity. Without us, and our forefathers of glorious memory, their commerce would vie with your own. I appeal to your own writers on commerce for the truth of this affertion. Her fleets and armies would make her formidable; witnefs her natural advantages of every kind. She wou'd now, as formerly, be foremoft in fcience. Arduous indeed was the tafk of extirpating literature entirely from among them, for the very loweft and poereft of the wretches have a ftrange hankering after learning, not to be found among the fame defcription any where elfe; and, what is fcarce lefs alarming, they have a fingular capacity too for fcientific purfuit. To pick up a little learning, there is no hardfhip to which they will not fubmit, nakednefs, hunger, and toil.

"Is Ireland this day a prey to bigot fury, fanguinary politics, and religious faction? It is afcendancy challenges the merit of lighting up the torch of difcord. After having prepared the elements of confufion and civil ftrife, by an elaborate well connected fyftem of perfecuting ftatutes and oppreffion, religious bigotry, the fure and ready inftrument of civil difunion, would, ere now, have been extinguifhed, but for the foftering care of intolerance, which plied it conftantly with its proper food, ignorance and hatred. Perfecution fours the mind, provokes refentment and violent averfion to the opinions and perfons of the perfecutors, and difqualifies it for difpaffionate enquiry. Opinions pretended to be enforced in that unwarrantable manner, have no chance of a fair hearing, or impartial examination, while ignorance renders the inveftigation nearly impoffible; the fufferers are prompted naturally enough to reject the inftruction that comes accompanied with malice and oppreffion, becaufe the intereft of truth and virtue cannot infpire the injuftice which they condemn.

"Thus placed in the hoftile relation of Tyrant

and Slave, of perfecutor and perfecuted, one fide claiming a monopoly of the good things of this world in favour of their ftate religion ; the other arrogating to themfelves the exclufive enjoyment of the kingdom come, as the reward of their prefent mifery. A coalition durable as fincere between parties thus inflamed againft one another, by the conflict of intolerance, and the conilict of interefts, is not to be apprehended. For thefe and name-lefs other fervices, you now propofe to requite us, by robbing us of our expected rewards, juft as we were proceeding to entail on ourfelves and pofterity the offices, honours, and emoluments of church and ftate, to the exclufion of fuch even of the fa-voured fect as had oppofed our meafures, at any time, through the monoploy of parliamentary reprefentation. What becomes of your honour and plighted faith, never to forfake us while we fup-ported you ? Alas! the Punic faith is revived once more ! What! take from us that conftitution, pro-vided by the wifdom of our anceftors, for the ac-commodation of you and us, at the expence of the wild Irifh ! ah ! if you feel no concern for the dif-may and defpair that would attend the difappoint-ment of fo many mercenaries, claiming the rewards juftly due to their exertions againft their country, in behalf of your fupremacy, in hopes of finding their private account therein ; at leaft ponder on the mifchiefs that may refult to yourfelf and to Bri-tain, from fo rafh and ungrateful a proceeding, your ftaunch and zealous blood hounds, may be driven by refentment, into an alliance with patriot rebels ; for, let me tell you, Sir, oh fure I need not inform you, that the men of our phalanx, how-ever they may degrade themfelves by cruelty and

treachery, they will not paffively bear to be de-
fpoiled of the wages of proftitution and barbarity.
Great crimes are feldom committed without great
profpects of advantage. Men do not fubmit to
lafting infamy for nothing. Traitors to their country, informers, fpies, butchers of their fellow-citizens, ravifhers of female honour, &c. ftifle remorfe,
which the feelings of nature awaken even in them,
by the powerful allurements of pleafure and gain.
Minifter to their paffions and their vices; they will
worfhip you in return; there is no crime fo abomi-
nable they will not deliberately plunge into; command them to fcalp or devour the corpfes of thofe
they murdered, to erect pyramids of fculls, &c.
you fhall be furprized at the alacrity of their obedience, provided the reward lag not behind. There
have been inftances of their biting the palpitating
hearts of the flain, and exclaiming while they de-
voured the cannibal repaft, *No food fo fweet as the
heart of a rebel.*

" But fhould they be cheated of their hire, none
fo untractable or vindictive; fpite would make them
patriots; Ireland would become free, and alas!
foon rival the profperity of opulent Carthage; you
would never again find in that country any party fo
entirely adapted for inftruments of your crufhing
and dividing policy; accuftomed to tamper with
confcience, which they facrifice at the fhrine of
ambition and lucre, they are proof againft its admonitions. They have learned, in the corrupting
traffic of boroughs, corportions, parliament and
law, to leave the pedantic rules of morality, to
guide low grovelling mortals unverfed in ftate affairs.

" There are, indeed, others of more rigid prin-

ciples, good proteſtants, ſtaunch loyaliſts, ripe e-
nough for any miſchief, for the *love of God*, and
the good of their ſouls. Theſe may be retained at
a trifling expence. But for the others, the deſign-
ing and ſelfiſh partizans, who are not to be ſtimu-
lated by empty ſounds, but calculate the profits
of their crimes————(Here a gentleman preſent at
the debate interpoſed)—" Come, come, Mr. Iriſh-
man, no independence, no republics; king, king,
for ever; king is needful thing; king is God's vi-
car, Lord's anointed; anointed, do you ſee; biſhop pour oil upon his head; Iriſh wicked; very
wicked; what! what! have no ki g! compoſe,
magine king's death! force and arms! fooliſh Iriſh!
Iriſh without king! no biſhop! no ſou! gees to hea-
ven! he, he! no graſs grow, no corn; he! no
meat or drink! all loſt; every thing dear, he! Engliſh people very good; fine, fine people; keep
the kings upon the thrones; pay the great taxes;
every guinea to the laſt, for the king, that make
them all live; muſt hang the Iriſh! hang 'em up!
he, he! Engliſh fight for king; pay for king: pray
for king; ſing God ſave king; love king in their
hearts; worſhip king. Americans good boys a-
gain; fight for king. What! what! loſe Ireland!
no, no, muſt not loſe Ireland; there we have fine
fat cows, great big cows; and clever bulls, Iriſh
bulls! he, he! what ſay you, Pitt?

Hereupon the vizier addreſſing himſelf to the
aſcendancy chief, " You, and your friends, and
whoever elſe cannot ſafely be treated with neglect,
ſhall be provided for; as for the rabble of your
party, we may ſafely leave them to the management of their clergy, who will work them up to
our purpoſes, by plying their ante-popiſh zeal with

caustic dofes of controverfial invective." The bri-
gain ftruck; the cabinet broke up; and poor Ireland is loft for ever!

It is then the duped afcendancy bigots, will have
caufe to lament their fatal miftake, when they fuf-
fered themfelves to be hallooed like blood-hounds,
to worry their fellow-citizens, and crufh the patriot fpirit, for the gratification and benefit of their
defigning leaders, who now difpofe of them like fo
many head of cattle. In the articles of compenfation for battering away irrecoverably the rights
and profperity of the country, they are forgotten,
and left to fhare its ruin and poverty, fince they
would not its greatnefs and independence.

Orangemen, take a profpective view of the
bleffings you have prepared for yourfelves and your
children. The proprietory of the kingdom gone to
refide in England, to attend the bufinefs in parliament, the court, &c. All who afpire to the career of ambition and honour, or the pleafures of
elegant and rational fociety, or the amufement of
a great court and capital; emigration will become
the tone; and it will be quite unfafhionable, odious,
to refide in Ireland; enough to give a fine bred la-
dy the vapours. The vulgar provincialifm of Irifh
airs, accent, &c. &c. will be avoided like the
plague; to efcape the flighteft taint, or even fuf-
picion of it become an important concern; a per-
manent refidence in London or Bath will be the
indifpenfible with every fquire and fquirefs who
can afford it.

On the other hand, a beggared, deferted province can have no inducements to retain the opulent, and fuch as cannot afford the expence of that
fafhionable country, will fend their children thi-

ther for education, or rather fend their wives thither to be delivered, that their offspring may avoid
the difgrace of being born here, and educated
quite free from any Irifh impreffions; untainted
with the candour, affability, and hofpitality that
diftinguifhed that degenerate people ; but trained
up in the genteeleft prejudices againft every thing
Irifh, he will be early taught to treat the country
of his fathers with injuftice and contempt. Thus
almoft the whole rental of the kingdom will be
fpent in foreign parts, to enrich pampered England ; trade and the arts, deprived of their cuftomers, muft follow ; the capital will fall into ruin ;
agriculture will dwindle, &c. Population muft wafte
away, and refign the foil to bullocks and fheep.
The vaft fums laid out in improving the capital,
and its vicinity, in the conftruction of canals, quays,
bridges, roads, the melioration of harbours, rivers ; in the encouragement of agriculture, arts,
fifheries ; in the endowment of colleges, fchools,
hofpitals, &c. is all loft ! expended in vain ! all
will become next to ufelefs. The halls of the univerfity and the four courts will be filent ; the bud-
ding gems of fcience and genius will droop and
die, and the future ftate of Dublin may be com-
pared to the ruin of Babylon, as predicted by Ifa-
iah. " And Babylon, the glory of kingdoms, the
" beauty of the Chaldee excellency, fhall be as
" when God overthrew Sodom and Gomorrah ;
" it fhall never be inhabited, neither fhall it be
" dwelt in from generation to generation ; but wild
" beafts of the defert fhall lie there, and there
" houfes fhall be full of doleful creatures, and owls
" fhall dwell there, and fatyrs fhall dance there,
" and the wild beafts of the ifland fhall cry in

D

" their defolate houfes, and dragons in their plea-
" fant palaces, &c."

An expectation will be raifed, that Englifh capital and manufactures will find their way hither,
enticed by the cheapnefs of provifion and labour·

Very improbable indeed. There are far more
powerful inducements to retain them at the other
fide ; the vicinity of the great emporium of the
world ; the fountain of credit, trade, &c. &c. The
mutual dependance and fubferviency of all the arts
and manufactures, each miniftring to and borrow-
ing from each, or neceffary inftruments, or ufeful
hints, or ready circulation, &c. &c.

The manufacturer derives immenfe advantages
from the co-oporation of all the parts that form the
complex and ftupendous fabric of Englifh trade,
capital and credit, which a man of known probi-
ty and ability may command almoft to any a-
mount ; abundance of expert hands, and ingenious heads, the utenfils, machinery, proceffes, &c.
employed in high perfection, expeditious, cheap,
and every day receiving new improvements ; the
habit of induftry, fobriety and punctuality, preva-
lent among the laborious defcription ; the general
fpirit of enterprize and commercial fpeculation,
that turns every thing to account : thefe advantages more than counterbalance the difference in
the price of labour and provifions, and enable
the London or Birmingham manufacturer to un-
derfel the German or Ruffian. Any branch ex-
iled into Ireland, would fuffer more by its fepara-
tion from the living body, and vital circulation,
and harmonious co-operation of all the co-mem-
bers, the coefficient parts that conftitute the inte-
gral frame of a flourifhing commerce, than the

trifling difference in the price of provifion could poffibly compenfate.

Great indeed muft be the local temptations that could prevail on that calculating defcription, to renounce the vantage ground of their pofition. What would provincialed Ireland have to offer? An impoverifhed ragged population, with manners and habits not over-propitious to the commercial purfuits; obnoxious to the worft prejudices of Englifhmen; a country however fertile, drained by the tributary rents of a hoft of abfentees, and crufhed by a full participation of Englifh debts, and taxes, increafed with her increafing inability to pay them; no home market; none of the co-operating trades, &c. &c. In the teeth of fuch dif-couragements, will Englifh manufacturers come to refide among a people whom they have been taught to hate and defpife from their infancy, and whom, when they are very liberal, they call *femibarbarous*; *deftitute of induftry, punctuality*, and even *honefty, Credat qui velit non ego.* You will, Irifhmen, gain an inundation of taxes, and tax-gatherers. No more.

APPENDIX.

IT appeared eligible to delay publication, in order
  to notice an anonymous production in favour of
Union, which common fame aſcribes to the pen
of a Gentleman high in office. The matter and
manner are ſuch as beſpeak the well bred ſcholar;
and the quarter from which it has iſſued, leaves no
doubt of the project being far advanced, and au-
thorizes us to conſider ſaid performance as the beſt
defence the meaſure would admit, beſide the *ultima
ratio regum*, or the logic of canon law.

The Reader will find moſt of the arguments that
bear directly on the ſubject anticipated in the foregoing pages. Admirable to think, that odious
deteſtable thing called *Union*, is ſuddenly purified
from all its unnatural foulneſs, by the regenerating
breath of the Engliſh ſtateſman. The union of
Iriſhmen for Iriſh and national purpoſes, is loaded

with every opprobrious epithet that language or imagination could suggest; but the union of the fame people with Britons, for the purpose of entailing everlasting thraldom on their country to the latest posterity, has, by that very circumstance, received the expiatory *absolvo te* of the cabinet, glittering in all the grace and glofs of its new birth. It is the very Panaceum for all our complaints. Spilfbury's drops contain not more virtues.

Happy Ireland! did you feel the honour and felicity referved for you, in the clofe embraces of your friendly, humane, candid, liberal neighbour, John Bull! One blefling this writer enfures to you in his name, as the firft fruit of your clofer connexion; hear his own words: *There would be no danger of Ireland growing too powerful hereafter.* Granted. From the temptations of power and wealth we would be faved, by the kind provident care of our new mafters. But then our *barbarous poor*, unpolifhed people would be refined, &c. by our intimacy with the elegant, agreeable, focial, highly polifhed Englifh! ! ! What ftrange tales we are deftined to hear! Learn good breeding and politenefs from the churlifh, growling, and felfifh race of Englifhmen!

If it be a characteriftic of good manners to treat all neighbouring nations with rude infolence, and foul mouthed contumely, there we might learn; we have had abundant fpecimens of thofe humane and polite Englifh tutors, the ancient and modern Britons, Midlothians, Dunbartons, &c. &c. Their leffons will not be foon forgotten; for they have been written in our blood, by fire and fword, and all the rage of luft, and plunder, and military execution. May God preferve us hereafter from fuch teachers of civilization, as Englishmen have invariably proved themselves here. To civilize the *wild Irish* meant, in their language, to plunder and exterminate them. In the polite accomplishments of boxing, swearing, gluttony, rudeness, unfeeling avarice, &c. they stand unrivalled. Take a specimen of their elegant conversation and stile : *Nay, damn my eyes. God damn my eyes, face and nose. I'll be damned if. God damn my bloody eyes,* &c. &c. &c. Such are the flowers which cocknified Irishmen may borrow to adorn our isle !

However, did England surpass the courtly complaisance of Italy, or the gay urbanity of polished France, that were no reason why we should surrender our national independence. We may borrow improvements from our neighbours, without becoming their servants. How would England relish the proposal of being made a province to France, on the frivolous pretext of the superior politeness of the latter ?

We are told of the advantage of sending our children beyond the channel for education. If that be any mighty privilege, we may enjoy it without that fatal measure ; it would, in that case, grow to an alarming nuisance, as stated in the foregoing pages. Trinity College might certainly abide the competition, as far as it depended on solid and extensive learning, &c. But the seat of power and legislation, the source of honours and preferments, the splendid theatre of ambition, eloquence, &c. fashionable society, amusements, &c. would draw most of our opulent families thither, and fix the education of youth of distinction exclusively there. The hundred frivolities to which the varying fashion of the hour annexes the importance of first rate accomplifhments, fo indifpenfible for a young man, *du bel air*, would procure Englifh education a de-cided preference ; befide the convenience of living near their relatives, of forming and cultivating ear-ly connexions with the Englifh youth of diftincti-on, of hearing the great models of parliamentary and legal elequence, &c. &c.

Then indeed might Oxford and Cambridge ftile the Univerfity of Dublin *Our Silent Sifter*. Well but we are to have Irifhmen in the Britifh cabinet, and of courfe the policy of the empire is to receive a direction favourable to this country. The author means Englifhmen poffeffed of Irifh eftates. Such there are already, without procuring any material benefit for us. Families domefticated and refident in England from generation to generation, can be denominated Irifhmen in no other fenfe than the above. There is one grand confolation ftill be-hind; the Englifh are exceeding wealthy. So great is the redundancy of capital in that happy land, that they are at a lofs for objects of fpeculation, in the whole wide range of univerfal commerce and war. Therefore, as they have more money than they know how to difpofe of, they will charitably employ part in draining our bogs, and reclaiming our mountains. Good-natured fouls! Like the ufurer in Horace, they would fcheme plans of ru-ral improvement in December, and fly with their bags to 'Change-alley in January.

See the reafons previoufly adduced, to prove that Englifh capital would not flow fo copioufly up-on us as fome would perfuade. In fact the com-mercial enterprize of England will fpeculate on our raw materials, as heretofore ; but they will have no additional inducements to form fettlements, or eſtabliſh manufactures among us. For the ſame reaſons they will be as ready to ſpeculate on the produce of France, Spain, or Turkey, &c. Commercial avarice knows no principle of preference but ſelf-intereſt.

To the arguments contained in the firſt part I would add, that a luxurious elegance prevails more and more in manufactures, calling forth the aid of Science and the fine arts; of chymiſtry, botany, painting, deſign, &c. A delicate attention to the naſcent variations in faſhion is neceſſary to their ſucceſs; on which account the vicinity of the court and capital is a weighty conſideration.

When Paddy got a free trade, it was confidently affirmed, that Engliſh capitals would be veſted in manufactures here. Theſe fond expectations proved deluſive, as no doubt, in the preſent inſtance, they will, if people are ſilly enough to reckon on them. Is it likely that increaſe of taxes, of price of labour, &c. will add to the inducements of eſtabliſhing? Here we touch on the grand benefit we may certainly expect to reap from the projected union : a bountiful dividend of the *moderate* taxes and debt of England; our full proportion of no leſs a ſum than *five hundred million!* which, for aught we can ſee, may increaſe to a thouſand millions before the concluſion of this neceſſary war, if public credit can laſt ſo long.

The ſupporter of union tells us, how deſirable it would be for a young merchant, to be admitted to a ſhare in the firm of a wealthy extenſive trader. It might be ſo, if the firm were unincumbered, and the terms fair and reciprocal. But if the great trader were incumbered with debts beyond his ability, and the terms were the complete ſubjection and dependance of his affociate, I for one cannot fee the policy of joining his moderate, but comparatively unincumbered eftate, to the fplendid bankruptcy of his haughty neighbour, on the difhonourable terms of vaffalage, and menial fervitude to himfelf and heirs for ever. Were the profpects of lucre lefs equivocal, ftill I would not advife the furrender of our independence, our birth-right, for a mefs of pottadge ; but to fling away both honour and intereft at a ftroke, would be fomething worfe than the Irifh blundering bulls we are accufed of. Honour cannot be feparated from intereft, it conftitutes the out-works and rampart of every thing dear to the heart. In the language of Junius, " The feathers that adorn the royal bird, fupport him in his flight; ftrip him of his plumage, and you fix him to the earth." Once you have furrendered your palladium, with the citadel of your independent legiflature, you are at the mercy of every Britifh minifter, fit objects for experimental effays in the articles of government, taxation, &c.

The terms of the connexion may be new modelled, as it may fuit the caprice or convenience of your mafters, without your confent. It may be faid we have a ftrong pledge in the good faith of Englifhmen. Let the violated treaty of Limerick ftand the perpetual, but not folitary record of their *good faith* ; let the commercial reftraints, and other ufurpations againft the terms of our connexion anfwer.

On furrendering our ftaple, the woollen and other branches, they promifed us a monopoly of the linen manufactures. How have they kept terms dictated by themfelves ? By encouraging this branch both in England and Scotland ; by pur-

chafing immenfe quantities of Ruffian and German
linens, &c. Nay, the very act of incorporating
Ireland would amount to a breach of the public
faith with Scotland, by deftroying the proportional
weight of its reprefentatives in the legiflature. Let
keen-eyed Scotland look to that point.

A further advantage we are promifed from the
union, tranquillity and fecurity of property. This
feems plaufible enough. It is taken for granted,
that the factions here will be quiet when they have
nothing to fcramble for ; when every object of ambition and emulation is removed far away. This
is affuming the prophetic tone. Who can tell us
what the confequence would be of public difcontent repining at loft independence ? We have feen
two rebellions in Scotland fince the union took
place, which fhould compenfate the lofs of independence with perpetual tranquillity.

Prithee, is it from the rioters of Weftminfter, or
Lord Gordon's proteftant mob, the Irifh are to im-
bibe the meek fpirit of fubordination to the laws ?
Moft affuredly, England has not taught the nations
the leffon of paffive obedience and non-refiftance ;
the fpirit of independence which fhe formerly attempted to fubdue in America, and now combats
in France, is her own legitimate offspring ; to their
credit be it remembered, the Englifh of yore
would neither crouch to kings nor priefts, regard-
ing all fuch public officers, by whatever name de-
corated, as public fervants, refponfible for their
miniftry, and liable to be cafhiered for mifconduct,
as they frequently were. So much for the fpirit of
meek obedience we are, it feems, to learn from
a clofer connexion with that mettlefome people.
Here follows what the writer thinks a dexterous ar-

gument. In confequence of the union Ireland muft rife to the level of Englifh opulence, or England muft fink to the level of Irifh poverty; ergo, Ireland muft become as rich as England. I deny the confequence. The difproportion between the two countries may happen to be encreafed, not diminifhed by the meafure. Wales has not rifen to the level of England, nor Jamaica, nor Barbadoes, nor the Ifle of Man; and Old Sarum is a good deal behind London, notwithftanding the ftatiftic levelling power of legiflative unity.

Having exhaufted his rhetoric on topics applicable to us as a nation, the writer defcends to thofe minor interefts that divide our factions, religious or political. On thefe particulars he dwells with the fervor and complacency natural to a man eager to carry his point; and confcious of the ftrong ground on which he ftands, he addreffes party feelings with a confiderable degree of dexterity, well knowing that on their operation he muft ultimately rely for the fuccefs of his fcheme.

Sorry am I to confefs, that on this ground he is a formidable opponent; not from the intrinfic evidence or force of his reafoning, but from the infatuation and unhappy temper of the times; difclaiming the inhuman motive of reviving and inflaming the recent animofities of party, yet he contrives to touch on all the fubjects of ftrife that have divided and laid wafte this unhappy country. I felt humbled when I perufed that crafty appeal to thofe paffions that difgrace, and muft, if not checked, extinguifh us as a nation. The people are degraded indeed, to whom fuch language and reafoning are applied; with the view of inducing them to abdicate their independence, and part

with the precious dear-bought privilege of legiflat-
ing for, and taxing themfelves; they are fuppofed
the moft infatuated bigots that ever difgraced the
earth, incapable of bearing with each other, mu-
tually bent on each other's deftruction, and therefore incompetent to the functions of legiflation, indeed unworthy of enjoying the leaft particle of
freedom.

In the firft part of this pamphlet, the caufes that
perpetuate the hoftility of fects have been, I truft,
elucidated to the fatisfaction of any candid enquir-
er. It appeared that not difference of religion, but
oppofition to intereft, immortalizes bigotry. That
any general defcription of men, felected as objects
of civil disfranchifement, penalties, and perfecution, and marked out as objects of hatred and fcorn,
whether on account of any peculiarity of tenets,
religious or political, or any diftinguifhing features,
whether of colour, ftature, &c, would by that very
circumftance be embodied into an hoftile caft, and
the reaction of bigotry, direct and reflected, would
preferve the feeds of hatred, until the caufe be removed. Black men, and white men, and red men
will anfwer the purpofes of the old tyrannic policy, *divide & impera*, as well as religion. England
and France, almoft every ftate in Europe, have
been at fome period or another the theatres of religious factions; they have all in their turns been
convulfed by the fanguinary fury of contending bigotry. This truly evil and irreligious fpirit has either vanifhed, or been quelled in other countries;
why may we not be permitted to hope for our own,
the radical caufe of all the mifchief? The afcendancy of priefts over the civil power has declined,
and is declining; the extinction of both is retarded

among us folely by the arts of Britain. Oh! ill-natured felfifh Britain ! how long will you diftract us by your bafe intrigues? How long will your un-worthy policy arm fect. againft fect, friend againft, friend, neighbour againft neighbour, in unnatural parricidal warfare ? Will you never ceafe bribing one party with a pittance of the common fpoil, to hold in fhameful fubjugation and ruinous reftraint the other and more numerous portion ?

The abettor of union afks, Why may not Bri-tain, if fhe chufes, adopt the catholic inftead of the proteftant, as the inftrument of her fupremacy over Ireland? A very fair queftion. Pity he has not thought proper to folve it. It will not be ad-vanced by any one in the leaft converfant with mi-niftry, their opinions, or motives of conduct, that their religious prejudices determine the preference. No. They have affociated with popifh priefts, emi-grant and non-emigrant, with the pope and Turk, and would as cordially with his Satanic majefty, if he difplayed *vigour* and *decifion* in favour of the common caufe. What then has entitled proteftants to the difgraceful partiality of Britifh policy, and qualified them to be the undoers of the land of their birth? I anfwer, the fingle circumftance of their being the minority; were they the majority, they would feel as a nation; for the honour and in-dependence of their country, no paltry dividend of the fpoils of an impoverifhed and enflaved coun try would prevail on them to facrifice their rights, and forego their far more ample, honourable, ard fafe portion of the natural wealth and profperity, which the bounteous nature of the foil, and its hap-py fituation almoft forces on them, in fpite of the unwearied exertions of counteraction; they would not miscalculate so egregiously as not to know, that the half of a pound is better than the whole of a shilling; and that a shilling honestly earned, is better than a pound obtained unjustly.

The artificial power of government, supported by the power of numbers, would command respect, and make it unsafe to attempt upon their dignity or interest. This explains why numbers and power, property and no property, must be opposed to each other. The selfish monopolizing nation is jealous of our natural advantages; she dreads our rising prosperity and greatness; the natural resources she cannot extinguish, she labours to render them useless to us, and that unworthy purpose she can accomplish only through our divisions.

Alas! cruel England! take away your nonsensical ascendancy, your unjust monopolies, your vile machinations; leave us to the cool and sober reflection of our judgments; then we shall have equal rights, equal laws, a common interest, and a common country. Those distinctions that are preserved, only because they furnish pretexts and objects of injustice, will gradually melt away, and be dissolved by the breath of reason and philanthropy; then Christianity will not be disgraced by the horrid excesses of its votaries; excesses that argue more against it than a thousand syllogisms; no good tree bringeth forth bad fruit, &c. Why should England dread the prosperity of Ireland? Would she not benefit more from its wealth than from its poverty? Is not her commercial intercourse productive in the ratio of the opulence of her customers? But she would apprehend rivality, on collision of interest. Be just and fear not. Who thinketh no evil, suspecteth none. Rivality within the bounds of juftice, is falutary to nations and individuals; why dread hoftile collifion? Has not Ireland a fimilar intereft with Great Britain, to preferve the balance of power, and oppofe the lawlefs aggrandizement of any given power? Her conduct might furely be trufted to the impulfes of intereft, duty, and good fenfe. Why not command the fervices of Irifhmen through their feelings, their gratitude, their fenfe of propriety and honour? My countrymen, I truft, are not deftitute of thefe exalted feelings, nor difqualified to liften to their nobler fuggeftions. The line of true policy is before you; it lies in the ftraight path of honefty, not in the windings of ftate treachery. Minifters however are too cunning to purfue the fafe path of integrity; they muft difplay vaft ingenuity in governing by dexterous trick and fubtle management; or indulge their defpotic humours, by reforting to the clumfy and mifchievous inftrument of coercion. They love to govern by crooked means, and too much (let them not deceive themfelves) found policy can never be feparated from ftrict honefty.

By the eternal decree of fovereign righteoufnefs, iniquity never fails to defeat itfelf, and fooner on later reaps in difgrace and ruin what it has fown in malice and deceit. By the fame adorable power it is ordained, that the inftruments and objects of crime become, in their turn, and in due feafon, the inftruments of punifhment. He has read hiftory to very little purpofe, who has not feen thefe eternal truths difplayed in the ftory of the nations, whofe records have been tranfmitted to pofterity.

But to return to our union. He has recourfe to the ftate bugbears, about the infecurity of protef-

tant property lay and clerical, should the catholics
succeed in their demands. His arguments amount
to this. Nine-tenth of the property is in the hands
of the protestants; the catholics are more numerous, therefore if the house of commons were
thrown open to them, they would there have the
majority, and ——what and ?——Will you guess,
courteous reader? Why they will proceed imme-
diately to strip themselves of their own property,
for the great majority of such catholics as could
pretend to the honour of a seat, derive from them
very protestants, either by lease or purchase, their
titles to their actual possessions. In favour of
whom would they make this unprecedented sacri-
fice? Where is the rightful heir? Fion Mac Cuil,
or Goll Mac Morna O'Nial, or Mac Cuirnay? We
should enquire into the titles of the Milesians themselves; ancient as they were, the island was occu-
pied before them. In all conscience, we should
ascend to the preadamites! It is shameful to ob-
trude such exploded nonsense on the patience of
the public. When the catholics formed the majority in as well as out of parliament, they attempted
no such thing. When they had it very much in
their power, and confiscations were recent, enormous, and in many instances flagitious robberies,
the rightful owners were in great part then living;
yet no intreaties on their part, no, not the tears,
and ruin, and despair of so many respectable families of their communion, destroyed by Strafford
of infamous memory, could induce them to oppose
the royal authority, though so prostituted to their
ruin; fearing from the republican temper of Britain, the constitution might be destroyed by their
endeavours for redress; they perished in support

of the Britifh conftitution, as the Vendeans have done in our day, in fupport of their king. Is it probable thofe who did not avail themfelves of their fuperior opulence, numbers, and majority in the legiflature, to conteft the recent titles to forfeit-ed eftates, that the fame, I fay, with nothing in their favour but numbers, fhould revive chimerical nonentities, to the unhinging their own fecurities? But ftill farther, it is utterly impoffible they can have a majority, nor even any thing approaching to an equal number in the legiflature, unlefs it can be fuppofed, that one hundretdh part of the national property can have more influence than the remaining ninety nine.

It is afferted by men of undoubted weight, that univerfal fuffrage would not free us from undue influence at elections. In thefe tranfactions men are guided by their temporal, not fpiritual interefts. Farmers would generally vote for their landlords, and artizans for their employers, without minding their catechifms. I know of no fhopkeeper who would bate a farthing in the price of his goods, in confideration of his cuftomers religion. The lefs party diftinctions are noticed by law and policy, the lefs will men be influenced by them in their dealings with each other. It is notorious, that the republicans would confider the conceffions of the catholic emancipation and reform as the moft compleat defeat. Rightly judging the prefent conftitution would be ftrengthened by the coalition of catholic and proteftant interefts. If they liftened to republican doctrines, it was becaufe their demands of incorporation was fcouted with difdain, and the refufal accompanied with a denunciation of eternal oppofition to future conceffions. This proceeding was not politic, becaufe neither wife nor honeft; they fhould have remembered, that in Pandora's box hope was left at the bottom. Heated by the conteft, and by the fpirit of the times, defpairing of their rights through the conftitution, they hearkened to thefe republican doctrines, which have no very natural alliance with their ecclefiaftical inftitutions. It was not the fociety in Back-lane, but the fociety in College-green that gave the rapid impulfe to the great majority of Irifhmen towards democracy. The meafures then rejected would ftill prove falutary; it is never too late to act rightly. But fhould it be given up as impracticable, I fee no alternative but an union. It is proved that danger to the proteftant intereft is chimerical.

ift. Becaufe the catholics have not the will, when they had the power, and the claimants were living, and the juftice of the claims evident in numerous inftances, and the affertion of thofe claims popular and plaufible. They acquiefced in the transfer of property; and now, that all circumftances are reverfed, and their power, even with a full participation of rights, but a fraction in the ftate, who but an ideot would apprehend any danger from their emancipation, with a proteftant king, and lords, and a majority in the commons, from the neceffary influence of property, in the proportion of at leaft ten to one, and the probability that a catholic ariftocracy would make common caufe with their proteftant colleagues and compeers, in preference to democracy of their own perfuafion? If any fuch principle could furvive the reftoration of the conftitution, as I am certain it could not, I can fee no danger in emancipation and reform, but much caufe of apprehenfion, in leaving the people

of Ireland difcontented either with or without an
union.

As for the danger to the church eftablifhment,
it cannot proceed from the catholics, as we have
feen, it is only by proteftants that it can be over-
turned. A modification of tithes, which is now
held forth as a rider to the union, would, without
fuch a meafure fatisfy the public on that head, and
fecure their livings to the clergy. The queftion,
in that cafe, would reft entirely between the incumbent and the landlord ; the interefts of agriculture would not be affected ; but let them look to
the confequences of an union. What muft dimi-
nifh population, and the value of land, cannot add
to the value of their livings.

As to the queftion of eftablifhments, as neceffary to the prefervation of religion, the hiftory of
religion is the beft folution. Chriftianity was pro-
pogated independent of fecular rewards ; it owes
nothing to eftablifhments, but abufes that have cor-
rupted it. The diffenters and catholics have fub-
fifted without ftate alliance ; why not the church of
England ? It is conferring very little honour on
that true religion, to fuppofe it cannot be preached
or believed, unlefs fupported by temporal power,
and large bribes to teachers and believers. What
a frail bantling muft it be, not to endure the
wholefome climate of equal juftice, and impartial
enquiry ? No, it muft be fwathed in flannels ; nurfed
by the ftate, kept very warm and comfortable in
the foft lap of luxury ; pampered with goodies ;
ftill the ricketty creature keeps fqualling, alarming
the family, its life is always in danger. But it would
be leaving religion to chance to deprive it of eftablifhment. How long will man be more cun-

ning than his maker? He that framed human nature, knew how to adapt his revelation to its wants and capacities; and trusted to its native beauty, simplicity, internal evidence, and powerful appeals to the best feelings of our nature, for its efficacy and undecaying virtue. Surely this was not throwing it abroad like a destitute orphan, deriving a precarious existence from casualty. A religion of human invention, must depend upon human policy for its short-lived existence. Every plant that my heavenly father hath not planted shall be rooted out. The repeal of the test act is maintained as another inconvenience attendant on reform. Where could be the mighty harm, if parliament had nothing to do with voting creeds, forming test acts, or inflicting penalties on non-conformists? Parliament owns it fallibility in spiritual concerns. Is it not inconsistent with that confession, to assume dominion over men's consciences, and punish them for not believing what may chance to be erroneous? In the science of taxation they may claim precedence of the council of Trent, the pope's conclave, or the convocation; but the art of creed-making, or voting articles of faith, should be relinquished to those whose peculiar profession qualifies them for the office. One might be a good member of parliament, and an honest man, though he should believe an article more or less than thirty nine.

Lastly, he addresses himself to the Irish legislature in terms which, from any other quarter, would be treated as seditious. He reproaches them rather in oblique terms with venality and corruption; with sacrificing the interests of their constitution to those of England; he says they were at least liable to the imputation. That may be true, but that is a reafon for reform, not for abolition. How would the British legiflature relifh fuch logic ? Muft it too be abolifhed? Undue influence is imputed to it. This feems fomewhat Jacobinical; it founds peculiarly hard and ungracious, as coming from the fame quarter whence the feduction and bribe originated; it is imitating the tempter of mankind, who is faid to be the accufer of fuch as he allures into his toils. *The connexion has been tried in various fhapes; and has invariably been found inadequate to the purpofes of good government. Therefore we fhould try the effect of an union.* Fine logic ! our partnerfhip with Britain has hitherto proved difaftrous, therefore we fhould refign the entire management of our affairs into her hands. A different conclufion might be drawn by the fame, viz. and therefore we fhould break up the partnerfhip, for if we were cheated and robbed while we were co-managers, through the purchafed negligence or treachery of our clerks, what chance remains of juftice when the fole and exclufive ftewardfhip is vefted in our fraudulent partner, without any obligation of rendering an account ? Another alternative remains, viz. to amend the terms of the connexion, and employ honeft clerks, who will give good fecurity, and render a faithful account of their dealings. A long ftring of precedents is prefented to us at the outfet, of fome nations who united, and others who feparated. That was their concern. They might do fo or let it alone, as beft fuited their fancy. In no inftance alledged, were the parties uniting feparated by an eternal, and often dangerous barrier, as we are. What moft furprizes me in this collection of precedents, is to fee French fraternization quoted as a fit precedent to juftify the union. From the ufual language of minifters, one fhould be led to think, that French rapacity furnifhed topics for reproach, not models for the imitation of our principled ftatef-men. Their quarrel now appears to be not with the deed, but the agent; yet the French themfelves have dealt more liberally with their allies; they left to the Dutch, Helvetic, and Cifalpine republics, their feparate exiftence, legiflatures, and directo-ries, &c. Legiflators of Ireland, you are called up-on to abdicate your ftations, on the plea of difho-nefty, or incapacity, or both. Will you plead guilty? will you fubmit? Shame upon you if you defpair of refuting the charge, by one honeft ef-fort; by removing the caufes of complaint; by re-forming the fyftem which fubjects you to thofe im-putations. The fault lies there rather than in the individuals. Remember that the honour and dear-eft interefts of yourfelves and country are now in your hands; beware how you transfer the power over thefe mighty concerns to foreign hands; you cannot lawfully overturn that conftitution, with the temporary adminiftration of which you are folely invefted; you cannot vote away the franchife which has created you, nor decree that as a province, you have received as an imperial independent kingdom, no more than the Englifh parliament can vote Eng-land an abfolute monarchy, or decree an union with France.

F I N I S.

www.ingramcontent.com/pod-product-compliance
Lightning Source LLC
Chambersburg PA
CBHW021555270326
41931CB00009B/1222